Late Autumn Sunlight

©Jardine Press 2001
Text © Martin Newell
Linocuts © James Dodds
ISBN 0-9539472-3-8

Late Autumn Sunlight

East Anglian Verses

by
Martin Newell
Linocuts by James Dodds

Jardine Press
2001

Contents

Introduction

An introduction, in fact, to a pair of collabora-
tionists who need no introduction. There cannot
be many parts of Britain where a local scene is
so well caught by poet and artist together. Were
it not for Martin Newell and James Dodds
today's East Anglia, and especially coastal
North-East Essex, would, like so many places, be
identified in the usual generalised terms of a
commuting area, plus some inviting tourist lan-
guage. But they will have none of this and
between them they have for a long time now
revealed the true nature of their homeland.
Martin Newell casts a protective eye over it.
There is nothing he cannot see and nothing he
cannot value. Although his vision is proprietorial,
he wants to share it. He has a genius for relating
the past to the present and not making all kinds
of things sound out-dated. His poetry is an
inventory of the region. He does not deal in "by-
gones" but in what connects. He is affectionately
caustic, witty and moving, a great local voice
which, via a stream of work in *The Independent*, is
listened to far and wide. He has always possessed
a sad ear for decline, for the running-down but
not the vanishing of things, and *Late Autumn
Sunlight* is a subject which suits him. It is wry,
funny, profound, a signpost to what could so eas-
ily be missed, wonderful sights, unique detail,
views which change the reader's perspective.
Which is what poetry is for.

Martin Newell could not have found a better
sharer of his vision than James Dodds. His
strong lino-cuts provide a perfect accompani-
ment to the words but rightly do not attempt to

illustrate them. Where the poet lists the real natives, the real activities of his corner of the world, the artist takes its harbours back to their essentials of shipping, storytelling, worship and domesticity. The populations of Aldeburgh and Wivenhoe are captured — walled-up, almost — between soil and sea. James Dodds also captures that freedom of the coast which makes sailors and fishermen another race. Both he and Martin Newell have a wary delight in local legends and *Late Autumn Sunlight* contains an extract from *Black Shuck*, to my mind a masterly re-telling of Eastern England's ghostly dog tale. shuck makes the Hound of the Baskervilles sound like man's best friend. The Newell version, with Dodds' pictures, is classic folklore and not to be missed.

Martin Newell's East Anglia tumbles about untidily, and points a finger at contemporary suburban standards. "Where is your soul?" he consistently asks. It is a question we have to answer. Is it in theme parks, in the tarted-up pub, at the rat-race? James Dodds' east Anglia is crafted in shipyards, farmyards and workshops, including the studios of its many artists. These were for him during his youth the places where skill came from hands, not words. A shipwright tells his apprentice, "I shan't say noth'n. *You* watch *me*" Newell and Dodds show how close they are in this first poem of their latest book. Their work is a combination of doing — and dreaming. Its pace is set to some extent by the poet's bike and by the slowed-up discipline of

the linocut. Nothing flashes past them or is
dashed off. There is contemplation. East
Anglians are returned to their roots, non-natives
given a delightful crash course on what these
coastal counties really are, on what made them.

Frequently local writers and artists go over the
old ground, the famous names and villages, the
much repeated customs and the tourist routes.
But not here. Martin Newell "sings" what both
East Anglia and its visitors would never see.
Modest lanes, ordinary people, not "characters",
the minutiae of life, marvellously personal sight-
ings of birds and plants are brought to our atten-
tion. He is a poet who says, "Look at what you
are missing!" James Dodds' work is an act of love
which incorporates a sturdy reality and legend.
His small coastal towns are anchorages for other
things as well as ships. Martin Newell has more
to say about the latest inhabitants than the old-
est inhabitants, and caustically. He sees East
Anglia under constant invasion by one horde or
another but able to hold its own. Humanity and
its detritus ultimately touches his heart. So here
is a two-man guide to the edges of Norfolk,
Suffolk and particularly to border-line Essex;
some poems and pictures which will make us
look at them differently.

Ronald Blythe.

Excerpt from **Shipshape**

In this old shed and that old shed
The sound of saw and adze was wed
To mallet, hammer, chisel, file
And sanding, sanding all the while.
Old boys who knew these waters here
Worked hard, spoke little, drank their beer
Knew every inlet, creek and quay
From Burnham up to Brightlingsea
Told Jamie, shipwright yet-to-be
"I shan't say noth'n. You watch me"
No more than that and graft concerned
Since this is how the craft was learned
In bits and bats and splintered wood
Until at last the boy made good.

In salt-marsh, towpath, shingle, mud
The Essex coast gets in the blood
In sea-kale, samphire, gorse and sedge
Which grows along the water's edge
Till further in, the wetland yields
To hazy summer mangold fields
The copses, hedgerows, tractor-tracks
With pallets of potato sacks
And houses hidden in the lanes
With Flemish roofs and weathervanes
The churches closed, or overgrown,
The flowers left in grass unmown
Except around a tended tomb
From long-lived bride to long-dead groom.

2

And here a heron, there a lark
A curlew calling in the dark
To break the silence in the night
When moonlight drapes the boatyard white
And as the tides drain back to sea
From many-channelled estuary
Exposing ribs, remains of ships
The mud devours, it smacks its lips
Till deeper down and all around
The estuary's digestive sound
On windless nights pervades the air
When nothing stirs the maidenhair
And marker buoys stare up and blink
To see the stars return their wink.

The tide bleeds out and in the mud
The ships squat down, deprived of blood
Their buxom hulls exposed to air
The shipwright's exhibition there
Is free of charge and on display
The whole year round and twice a day
The curves, the clinker boards and keel
— The parts the water helped conceal —
Are testimony to an art
Much older craftsmen helped impart
In whispers down the estuary
I shan't say noth'n. You watch me.
Until it reached the river beds
From these old sheds and those old sheds

Excerpt from **Black Shuck** —
The ghost dog of eastern England

The moon across the marshes
The lonely Essex Marshes
Through rotting bones of barges in the mud
The east wind calls the curlew
Who pipes his cry the same
As when the rivers ran with Saxon blood

Where Byrhtnoth, earl of Essex
A thousand years before
Lost Maldon to the seawolves, Olaf's Danes
And fell among the dying
The horses of his ceorls
Ran riderless, no hands to hold the reins

And Northey Island's slaughter
Was carried by the wind
To Tiptree, Totham, Tollesbury and beyond
When Essex was the frontline
And Saxons clashed with Danes
For forest, field, hanger, creek and pond

And then along the causeway
Did Shuck come slinking out
To snuffle round the bodies of the dead?
Their shattered swords and shields
Their corslets oozing gore
And only ravens circling overhead

For from these misty marshes
These sucking, popping marshes
The Dog jumps up and soundlessly goes by
To parish, copse and crossroad
Through churchyard, lane and field
Then you, or someone close to you may die

5

Thorpe Market

The bric-a-brac and gaudy tack
Of any generation
Are sold for pennies not for pounds
At Thorpe-le-Soken station
And kept in circulation

The portrait of King Edward swings
In creaking celebration
And peels by the public house
At Thorpe-le-Soken station
In which they serve libation

Then plant and flower auctions
In rusting iron sheds
Are filled with Essex faces
On weathered turnip heads
From Clacton or from Toosy
With their end of winter colds
Who bid at Thorpe-le-Soken
For a box of marigolds
At one pound-eighty? Eighty-five?
Ninety, do I hear?
They stick at one pound-ninety
And sod the auctioneer
Who glances over half-moon specs
With keen and practised eye
At hardy annual gardeners
Who won't be hoist so high

And paperbacks laid up in stacks
Defying your concentration
Are found on trestles ten-a-pound
At Thorpe-le-Soken station
Some still in publication

The prices paid for literature
Immune here to inflation
Where Barbara Cartland lies with Joyce
At Thorpe-le-Soken station
For your imagination

But despite the April sunshine
There's an easterly which wields
A cutting edge to chill you
From the Thorpe-le-Soken fields
And there beneath the conker tree
In quiet resignation
The traders turn their collars up
At Thorpe-le-Soken station
And curse their occupation

The maltings by the railyard
The legend says it plain
Make malt for Double Diamond
You'll read it from the train
You can smell it in the market
You can taste it in the rain
And it lingers in your nostrils
Till you're nearly home again

Then market women's wartime eyes
Are closed in concentration
To tally takings in the pub
By Thorpe-le-Soken station
A tricky operation

And I may have a drink or two
Of devil's embrocation
I like to watch the trains go by
At Thorpe-le-Soken station
And miss my destination.

7

The Corner Shop

Barton Stores as run by Pat and Gordon
Beside the railway bridge, a corner shop
Sold matches, household soap and coal
Bin bags, candles, kitchen roll
The things without which normal life might stop.

And after clocks went back in late October,
In tea-time traffic of the afternoon
A scent of ripened Cox's
Met flames from burning boxes
And rose to reach a pale grapefruit moon.

Halfway down the High Street, summer mornings
Pat's dulcet voice would ring to rout the birds
Her old pronunciation
Quaint to a population
Already drowned in Estuary words.

But lemons, pomegranates, limes
And Spanish chestnuts, clementines
Egyptian spuds, African grapes
From stony hills and sunny capes
Whose violet skies and white-flecked shores
Were worlds away from Barton Stores
Could bring a taste, a scent, a spray
Of summer on a winter's day.

Then on a blustery Sunday in the springtime
The shop filled up with weekend roasting smells
While sailors headed seawards
And drinkers ambled quay-wards
In cherry blossom snow and churchyard bells.

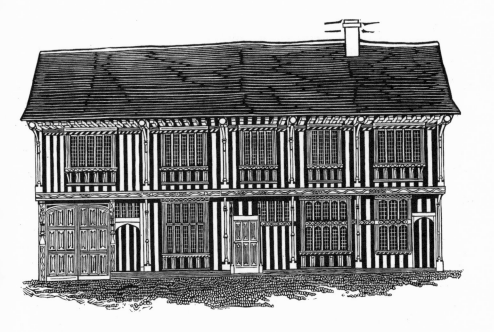

So ended half a century — and an era
The rueful moments of the closing day
And as the shop quit trading.
A ghost pulled down the shading
And watched a chunk of England fall away.

Warriors —

on finding the body of a Saxon chief and his horse
at a Suffolk airbase

A Saxon chieftain and his horse
Lay undisturbed in chalky ground
For fourteen hundred years or so
And slept the centuries away.

Much later, over farms and fens
Around a Suffolk air-force base
A younger German warrior flew
But fell to earth and lost the day.

"Well met", the Saxon soldier said.
"We've changed a bit since oxen carts
Though not so fast you'd notice it.
They take their time around these parts.

Where warriors younger now than you
Still gird themselves for battle zones.
Lie down young flier, the day will come
When men will marvel at your bones."

To A Postmistress Upon Retiring

The march of time went past the place
Its staples, pens and paperclips
Dockets, forms in duplicate
Postal orders, stamps and glue
Aged twenty-six, she took the shop
Way back in nineteen forty-two
When land girls were her customers.
The airmen, soldiers, farming men
And chaps with different accents
Sent letters home to lonely wives
As warplanes raked the Norfolk skies.

In 'forty-five, the boys came home
'Forty-seven, froze for weeks
Starving birds tapped window panes
And rationing was still in place

Through the dreary flooded fifties
Headscarved women, men in caps
Blazing skiffle summers, bees,
Telegrams on motor bikes.
Whitsun weekend, 'sixty-four,
On scooter run to Sheringham,
A lost patrol of London mods
Who puttered slowly past her door

In all that time and all those years
Of Christmas cards and sisal string
She'd license dogs and wirelesses
Motor cars and t.v. sets
Her weighing scales, arithmetic
And common sense were all she had.

Then half a century on or so
Up comes bold Efficiency
Who won't leave well enough alone
And says she must be 'putered-up.
Hard-disk, screen and god-knows-what
Can't be doing with all that.
Pen and paper did the lot
"Wun't be druv." She shut the shop.

* *"Wunt be druv" in the last line, is old Norfolk dialect
for: "won't be driven."*

The New Rural Vision

As I strode out one evening
In stockman's coat and hat
Genuine. Obtained from magazine.
I saw a host of houses
In yonder far-off fields
A place no longer designated green

The ranks of parked Hyundais
Gleamed bright on cobbled drives
With paintwork which no mud had ever splashed
In spears of fractured lamplight
From Pullman-curtained rooms
Where Tweedy met with Twee and quietly clashed

The claggy, rutted farm-tracks
Were strewn with bark and chip
Directions arrowed blue on wooden posts
While in the middle-distance
A phalanx of kagouls
Advanced upon the weekend-homes of hosts

A re-skilled border collie
Stood counselling the sheep
Assistance now the term, not Rounding Up
Liaising with Team Leader,
A "motivated" ram
Who formerly had held the job of Tup

A cockerel with a contract
Laid out in simple terms
Restricting crowing hours from ten 'til four
Perched sullen on a hen house
A bandage on his beak
And scanned the thing for any legal flaw

14

And as I wandered further
I chanced upon some trees
Now clearly marked an Ancient Woodland Site
I hadn't really nailed them
As anything but Woods
Though had they not been signposted, I might

And everywhere were warnings
To farmers and their kin
Forbidding muddy tractors on the road
"Please bag and bin your cowdung
And keep your sheep on leads."
New Labour says:
Respect The Country Code.

The Cycle Path

On a bicycle in winter
Back to Wivenhoe alone
When the smoky Rowhedge rooftops
Through the mist across the Colne
Are forgotten Saxon farmsteads
And the cattle stand like stone
On a still day in December
At the turning of the tide
With the fading roar of traffic
As the Hythe is left behind
For the patterned frosty woodland
Where the leaf-veins in the mud
Are the skeletons of fairies
Delicately strewn around
Then the only living sound
Is the wingbeat of a swan
As it flaps its way upriver
Past the moorhens in the sedge
To a white armada waiting
Silent at the water's edge.

On a bicycle in summer
In the horny pagan heat
Racing with a pleasure steamer
Where the rail and river meet
As a woman on the sun-deck
Sees the cyclist on the path
And she smiles, waving madly
Till he disappears in trees
Where the splinters of the sunlight
Splash the hawthorn leaves with gold
And the hollow-way is dappled
Where the burning ball has rolled
When the winter lost a wicket
After spring came in and bowled
A bluebell haze, the smell of rain
The thunder of the London train
A ship's wash jostles driftwood high
The seagulls see the bikes go by
And shriek along the estuary
To Brightlingsea. To Brightlingsea.

The Shipyard

Bramble, Southernwood and Dock
Unsung among the rubble
Were the salvagemen and saviours
Of a shipyard long in trouble:

"Mr. Bramble," said his colleague
"Since these premises are ours,
Will you formally confirm it
In the trademark of your flowers?
Now the welders won't return here
And the riveters have gone
We must be about our business
As the summer's getting on."

"Mr. Southernwood, the matter
Of this concrete still remains
It may crack with your persistence
And I see you've made some gains
But we fight a losing battle
With the tyrant of the clock
May I venture you prevail upon
The strengths of Mr. Dock?"

"Mr. Dock, you've made some progress
Since removal of the cranes
If the rusty sun assists us
And the heavy summer rains
We could sign the final papers
And conclude this sorry case
Leaving Mr. Moon as watchman
When the winter's on the place."

The War Memorials Of Norfolk

Muffled within vastnesses of Norfolk
The dusty cough of half-forgotten names
Remembered by old men in market taverns
Who stare in flames

From Southrepps, Blickling, Corpusty or Bacton
From Matlaske, Stratton Strawless, Alby Hill
They straggled like a badly-drilled militia
And then lay still

The conflict bawled its challenge out so loudly
That even these quiet places woke and heard
The exclamation marks became memorials
For war, the word.

Weather-pitted now, they stand in churchyards
Or modest squares, behind grey posts and chain
The poppy wreaths in early winter sunlight
Turned pink by rain.

And over time, beneath that scarecrow skyline
Across flat fields they drifted back alone
Ghosts who haunted grieving, sea-eyed sweethearts
Their names in stone.

The Last Ferry

When the chestnut slopes are rusty
And the Roman River still
And the reeds the only sentinels
From here to Chopping's Mill
Since the spirits of the legionaries
All returned to Rome,
With autumn in the saltings
You will take the ferry home.

The last one of October
And the loneliest of the year
Past blackened ribs of barges
Where the only sound you hear
Is the bickering of seagulls
In a melancholy sky
And the coughing of the engine
At the season sculling by

Then the swans reclaim the jetty
As the ferry slips from sight
And the sun goes down with jaundice
In a burst of dirty light
Till the shimmer of the windows
From the houses on the hill
Sends a semaphore of sunset
To the crows at Chopping's Mill

And Anchor Hill lies dozing
In the smoke of Sunday fires
And the starlings sit like symphonies
Unplayed upon the wires
And the ferry skipper's silent
At the closing of the day
As the sun creeps out of Quay Street
And the boat is put away.

23

Modern Village Life

My bike-lights pry down shiny drives
When watery autumn evenings fall
Where faux-Victorian bollards stand
"Dunhagglin" Three hundred grand.

Intruder lights snap on at night
To bathe the place in stalag white
The witch-hat gable, weathercock
And mock-colonial schoolhouse clock

The carriage wheels built into gate
For barn converted into home
With panoramic window view
And weatherboards a deal too new.

That distant man who shut the bank
It's partly him you have to thank
For helping close the grocer's down
And drive their business out of town

Into the maws of superstores
Who bleed the village into sleep
You're going to need a car you know
A mudless four wheel? There you go

Essential for the darkened lanes
And best of all with bull-bars on
To guard against pedestrians
The cyclists and equestrians.

Now driving will be half your life
The surgery, post office, pub
And to your station miles away
Then ride-on mower, on Saturday

Your kids can haunt the village green
To numb themselves on nasty beer
Then out of minds, get out of hand
Before they move to bedsit-land

No shadows to disquiet you here
But ghosts of yokels on the road
A most exclusive residence
From In-Like-Flynn Developments

Severe Weather Warning

I gotta get along now
Thass time for me to goo
I woulda stayed on longer but . . .
I think thass goornta snoo

Thass got as far as Croomer
My auntie toold me soo
She telephooned especially . . .
I think thass goornta snoo

Me feet got coold this morn'n
And generally they do
Thass even if I'm workin' . . .
I think thass goornta snoo

The wind comes off Siberia
Then when it start to bloo
That tend to cut right through you . . .
I think thass goornta snoo

If that gets far as Aylsham
Then Norwich gets it too
And they'll knoo all about it . . .
I think thass goornta snoo

They got a foot last winter
That only goos to shoo
It happens to us moost years . . .
I think thass goornta snoo.

I think thass goornta snoo
I doon't jest think — I knoo
Doon't say I never toold you . . .
I think thass goornta snoo.
I do.

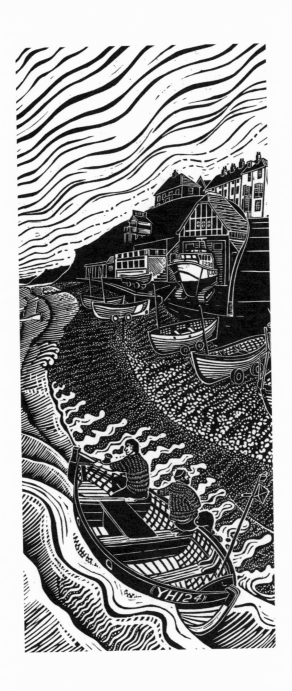

Frinton Rap
(Twelve-inch Crinkletown Mix)

Take a north EAST Essex TRAIN
Any wet DAY in the rain
And you change at THORPE for Kirby Cross
To a place where there's no CANDY floss
And you find yourself at FRINTON
Say wha?
I said FRINton
That's CRINKLETOWN where the old go to
To get aWAY from the likes of YOU
All the younger people LOOK bored
And dogs are BANNED from the GREENsward
And there are no PUBS
So no-one GOES
And they banned TRANSISTOR radios
Cos they've never heard of HIP hop
And there isn't any CHIP shop
And you can't CHANGE on the BEACH
And there's no BUS — so you're out of REACH
Of CLACton and WALton
If it's FRINton where you're coming from

Take a walk ROUND the AVENUES
Where there's blue RINSE in the PINK loos
And a Mathers-Platt   What is that?
It's a thief alarm on a GRANNY FLAT
There's a golf-club bar in CRINKLETOWN
But you can't get IN so you walk on DOWN
Past the BEACH huts and the WET rocks
And the crumbling wartime PILL-BOX
Which they built to keep the GERMANS out
And it must have worked — there are none about
So you stand THERE in the rain
It's a long wait till YOUR train
And you're cold BORED and thinking then
That the average age of a citizen
Must be N-n-n-n-Ninety. N-n-n-n-n Ninety
YO FRINTON

In Autumn Attic

Autumn came to Wivenhoe and slowly
Turned to ash the opal of the sky
Lovers took the last train out of Clacton
Drunken insects zig-zagged home to die.

Dutiful, the widow of the summer
Drifted through the apple-scented halls
This year's girl-most-likely-to was hanging
Rusty leaves on musty redbrick walls.

Westerlies, the stagehands of the season
Moved to shift the scenery away
Ruffled up the river down to Rowhedge
Drew the evening in to close the day.

Somewhere through the trees, a train to London
Sparked the overheads and slid from sight
Deeper in the woods a dog was barking
Someone on the station said goodnight.

Huddled in the pub, the early drinkers
Turned to see the window spanked by rain
Not to hear the calling of the curlew
Nor the ghosts of children in the lane.

The Funeral Of A Young Man

Wakes Colne White Colne
Earls Colne and Colne Engaine
Rainwashed green in early summer
As I cycle home again
Past the Chappel viaduct
Only memories will remain
Wakes Colne White Colne
Earls Colne and Colne Engaine

At the church — St Peter's Halstead
Cycle oil on trouser leg
Hymns were hardly made to measure
Service strictly off-the-peg
Always worse when it's a young man
Wheezed an older woman's voice
Yes, I thought — a decent send off
Pay your money take your choice
Sleep forever in the graveyard
At the eastern edge of town
Toxic yew trees, raised umbrellas
English weather — pouring down

He'd been chef and I'd been porter
Fond of cricket kind to me
Strange the things that you remember
Liked a song by Kiki Dee
Working in a narrow kitchen
Deafened by the radio
Shouted jokes and muddled orders
Table five? Away you go.
Different blokes on different wages
Makes me sorry now I think
He was bringing up a family
I was spending mine on drink

He'd been ill — I got a phone call
Now I'm cycling in the rain
Wakes Colne White Colne
Earls Colne and Colne Engaine
Had to borrow shirt and jacket
He'd be laughing like a drain
Wakes Colne White Colne
Earls Colne and Colne Engaine

Nineteen miles from home to Halstead
Nineteen miles then back again
Had the notion that exertion
Might stave off potential pain
Coming home I passed a postman
And we spoke as cyclists will
Asked me was I in a hurry
Only to be living still

Past the Chappel viaduct
Only memories can remain
Wakes Colne White Colne
Earls Colne and Colne Engaine

Under Milk Float . . . or Colchester Tales

In autumn — when fires are lit
I dream of broken fences in Cambridge Walk
Where conkers fall and spiky boys
Dog half-smoked spliffs en route to school

And by St Botolphs Circus
In Fagin's Den
I dream guitars and bullet-belted boys
And skinny girls who cry
In the amphetamine blue night

When the rain falls in Culver Street
The long-forgotten faces
From long-closed pubs
All asleep now walk beside me
Andy, Ted and Antoinette
Killed by drugs or motorbikes
Or coming home from parties
In the drunken dawn
All asleep now

In October — on Friday nights
I hear the hissing gas fires in Maldon Road
And the bedsit kids in thin black clothes
Who listen to The Mish — live on chips
Put their face on after work
Take their washing home to Mum
And spend all week in monochrome

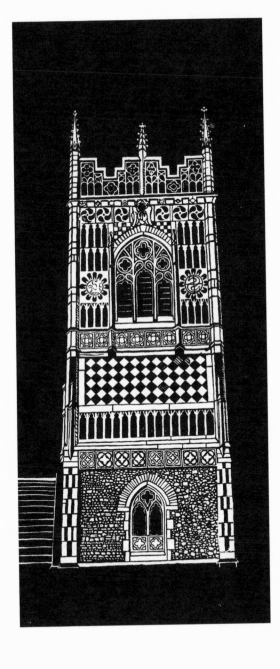

On Scheregate steps I met the devil
Standing by the paper shop
Tired now and middle-aged
Smoking in a tracksuit top

In autumn, when the sky is slate
And Priory Street is misty
I dream the teenage soldiers
Kissing chubby schoolgirls
In Artillery Folley
One kiss for now
And one for the Shankhill Road

And Old King Cole
Can't claim the dole
They caught his fiddlers three
But he does alright
In the Middleborough night
With his black and white TV

In the High Street — by The Hippodrome
In the orange afternoon
I dream the oyster feast
The town council
The red carpet
For celebrities
To gorge themselves in the town hall
While some bag-lady
Goes down with reality poisoning
Outside Sloppy Joe's

In autumn — when fires are lit
I take a teatime bus up Greenstead Road
With rabid steamy shoppers in their android clothes
Who dream of Telecom vans
And double glazing
Of shopping as religion
And cable television

Of rain-splashed windows in Lexden Road
Of half-term lovers on Hilly Fields
Of half-heard sirens in Castle Park
Of swishing car tyres down Brook Street
And listen to me now
In Autumn — when fires are lit
I dream

Dead In The Barmaid's Bed

Plywood coffin draped in sacks
Funeral feast of crisps and snacks
Poor man's Prozac — Special Brew
Massive turn-out, guests all knew
This is what the vicar said:
"Found him dead in the barmaid's bed."

Found him dead in the barmaid's bed
Lacy knickers on his head
What with all the gossip spread
Bound to raise his local cred.

Women tutted, men said, "Odd.
There but for the grace of God.
Not behaviour I'd endorse . . . "
Envious as hell of course.
Seeing him in that state of grace
Hard to keep a serious face
Should have legged it. Died instead
Found him dead in the barmaid's bed.

Man of Essex, thoroughbred.
Lead in pencil, gear in shed,
Brass in pocket, books in red,
Always kept his ferrets fed.
Found him dead in the barmaid's bed.
Found him dead in the barmaid's bed.
"Good owld buoy," they quietly said.
Found him dead in the barmaid's bed.

Horses Seen Through Trees

Some silver autumn morning
Remember days like these
As horses seen through trees

And in forgotten orchards
The ochre of the sun
And echo of a gun

A gale bends the birches
The elders crick and groan
The moon is smashed to pieces
In waters of the Colne
And autumn drags you home

The dead are reacquainted
With living they have known
Their half-remembered faces
In flowers, moss and stone
Ashes, earth or bone.

And if I die in early autumn
Light a fire boy — in the woods
Build it well and crack a bottle
Share out all my worldly goods.

And on some silver morning
Remember days like these
As horses seen through trees.

They Also Surf . . .
Beach Boys tributes pour in from Essex

If Brian Wilson came from Clacton
And not the U.S.A.
He'd have a very different post code
From Californ-I-Ay
You'd find it hard to imagine
The way it might have been
Had everybody gone surfin'
CO17

Well East Coast girls are hip
I really dig those coats they wear
And the Southend girls
When they eat their chips
They knock me out when I'm down there
The Essex farmers' daughters
Wear their jodhpurs far too tight
And the Maldon girls
With the way they spit
At their boyfriends late at night
But I wish they all could be
Saffron Walden girls

Well she hasn't got a car
And you can't rely on Eastern Region
And the Frinton over-sixties surfers
Had a pretty poor season
And they're rather short of happening bands
At the British Legion
But she'll have Fun Fun Fun
Till her daddy takes the tea-bag away

To Braintree —
Upon reading in a newspaper that its citizens were the ugliest in Britain

To Braintree Essex, where I hear
The local population
Were this week nominated
As the ugliest in our nation
Where bride may turn the groom to stone
Who'd courage to unveil her
While groom departs for honeymoon
With pig-net and a trailer.

Who slurs the name of Braintree
Rose of Essex, none serener?
The town is nice, the furry dice
In God's Own Ford Cortina.
We're honest here in Essex
If we've faults, then we admit 'em
But Braintree, ugliest? Not a chance . . .
No. That one goes to Witham.

43

Aldeburgh In January

Bitter sings the North Sea wind
That stabs through city clothes
And high the ragged herring gulls
Who screech
The leather-handed fishermen
Impervious to the cold
Will winch their boats up
On the shingle beach.

The artist isn't drawing
The writer doesn't write
But walk in silence
Through the winter day
While in the frozen distance
The ghosts of ships long sunk
Tall-masted haunt their hopes
From far away.

And all along the shoreline
The January tides
Come crashing through
The gateway of the year
To toast their unknown futures
In foam and muddy grey
A sea god flung a pint
Of dirty beer.

Bitter still the North Sea wind
And better in the pub
The smell of seafood pies
And Suffolk ale
The cosy lunchtime murmur
And scrape of forks and knives
To drown the doubts of those
Who fear to fail.

Our New Love, The Bus

Let's take the 78 in early winter
When all the oaks are turning gold
From Tenpenny Hill to Thorrington
In mid-November sunlight after rain
And kiss outside the Co-op here
Till 4.16 . . . and then 4.36 . . .

THEN AT THESE MINUTES
    PAST EACH HOUR

Until the buses all stop running
A full hour short of closing time.
From now on sweetheart, it is only us
The driver and that gum-chewing girl
Who meets her mates at Brightlingsea
A shivering, knackered office cleaner,
An old bloke back from seeing a son in jail,
And some kid talking draw-deals on a phone.
For these will be our fellow travellers
The very young, the aged and the car-less

And out along the estuary at tea-time
The headlamps dash the fields and lanes
And rake the stops where no-one waits
Who ever graduated to a car

DO NOT STAND FORWARD
    OF THIS POINT

Past a pub, a sign, a level-crossing
The new estate lit up like Lucozade
Deserted, but for hooded boys on bikes
A bell, a groan of brakes, a hiss of doors
Then back onto the rabbit-splattered road
The rattling draughty taxi's now our own

So let us take this 78 in winter
While all the world is busy driving home
One to each car and cursing at the traffic
Because apart from us and all these ghosts,

34 SEATED AND NINE STANDING

We may well find, at last, that we're alone.

The Dark Days Down To Christmas

The dark days down to Christmas paw
Like horses at an earthen floor
When all the ghosts of autumn pass away
And ragged squads of starlings fight
In firethorn trees in fading light
For orange berries brighter than the day

The dark days down to Christmas slip
As convicts from a prison ship
Down moonlit ropes and hawsers, one by one
And past the quayside through the lanes
With winter dragging on their chains
Peer into windows, envious of the sun

The dark days down to Christmas creep
As wolves around a pen of sheep
When people turn their collars up and sigh
A convalescent crescent moon
Comes drifting out mid-afternoon
To bid an old arthritic year goodbye

And down the drain these dark days spin
As kindling wood and paraffin
And sacks of coal and logs are fed
Into a spider-haunted shed
The garden tools with cobweb tines
And skeins of string on withered vines
Are vestiges left hanging on
As evidence of summer gone

The dark days down to Christmas call
In echoes to a flagstoned hall
Too early for the feast, they stay awhile
But each, an uninvited guest
Is dirty, cold and under-dressed
And slips away unmissed, in single file

The dark days down to Christmas wait
Like cinders cricking in a grate
Before the fire is raked, re-set and lit
And cheerless in their unmade bed
Glow only very faintly red
But give no hint of heat in spite of it

And yet with each dark day complete
Lighter and brighter grows the street
As frantic in the pubs and shops
The work speeds up — for soon, it stops
And in a lull between the two
The last day, having much to do
Though up till now, no time for thought
Allows a warming glass of port

And having set an hour free
Before the lights go on for tea
As ingots of old sunlight pierce the gloom
A ghost parade of days appears
With paler days from other years
Who reminisce in whispers round the room

The last day down to Christmas ends
Excusing all his sullen friends
Who slave until December twenty-third
Cut mistletoe, deliver parcels
Light the cottages like castles
Scribble cards and hardly say a word

Then having done their tasks they drift
As workers from a graveyard shift
The moment that each day has lost its light
Till wistfully, the last one goes
Ignites a candle, leaves a rose
And slips out softly, to the frosty night.

List of Linocuts